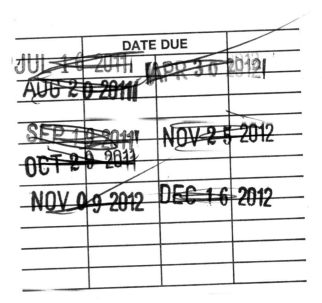

DATE DUE		
JUL 1 6 2011	APR 3 0 2012	
AUG 2 0 2011		
SEP 1 9 2011	NOV 2 5 2012	
OCT 2 0 2011		
NOV 0 9 2012	DEC 1 6 2012	

The Urbana Free Library

To renew materials call
217-367-4057

Airport

Byron Barton

HarperCollins*Publishers*®

Library of Congress Cataloging-in-Publication Data
Barton, Byron. Airport.
Summary: Describes and pictures what happens from
the time an airplane passenger arrives at an airport and
boards an airplane until the plane is in the air.
1. Airports—Juvenile literature.   [1. Airports]   I. Title.
TL725.B33 1982   387.7'36   79-7816 AACR2
ISBN 0-690-04168-3   ISBN 0-690-04169-1 (lib. bdg.)
(A Harper Trophy Book) ISBN 0-06-443145-2 (pbk.)

Published in hardcover by HarperCollins Publishers.
First Harper Trophy edition, 1987.
10 11 12 13 SCP 20 19 18 17 16 15 14 13 12 11

In buses

and in cars

people come to the airport.

They come to fly

Gates 1-6 →   Tickets   Baggage

in big jet planes.

In the waiting room

they sit and wait

while outside their planes

get loaded and checked.

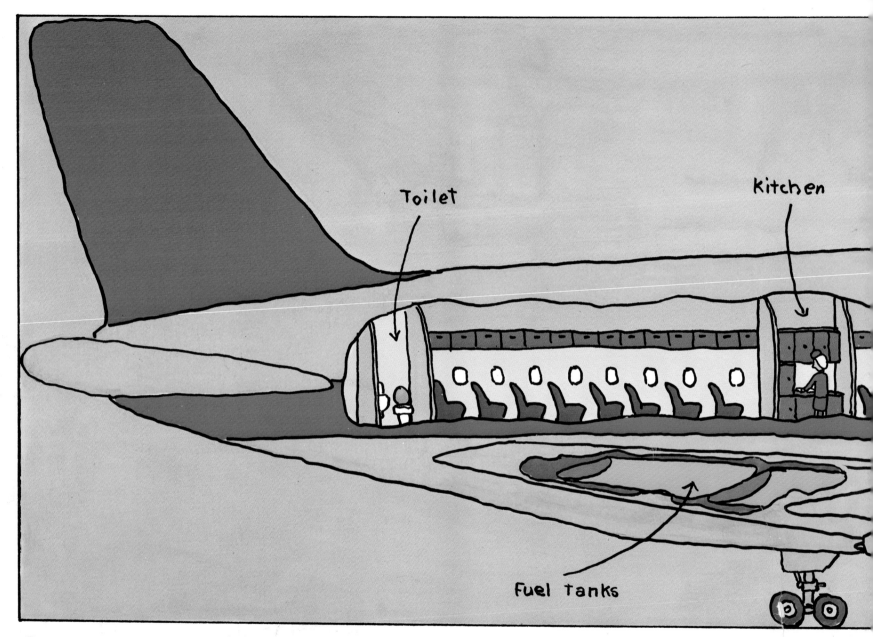

Suitcases go into the cargo hold.

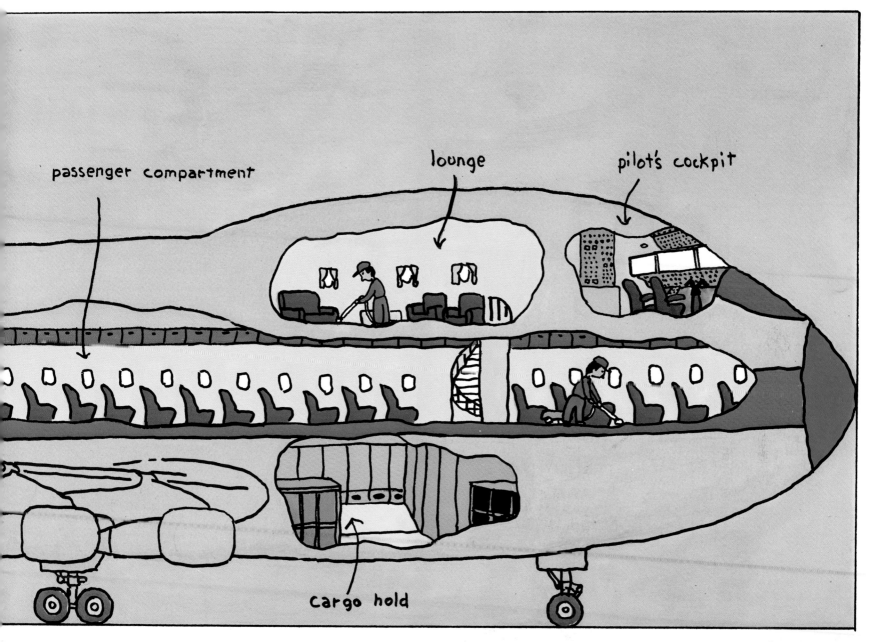

passenger compartment

lounge

pilot's cockpit

cargo hold

Fuel goes inside the wings.

Then the people

go on board.

They go inside

and find their seats.

Up front in the cockpit

the pilots get ready.

The control tower radios

when all is clear.

Buckle your seatbelts,

the flight attendant says.

The big plane starts rolling

slowly to the runway.

Control tower to pilot:

All clear for takeoff.

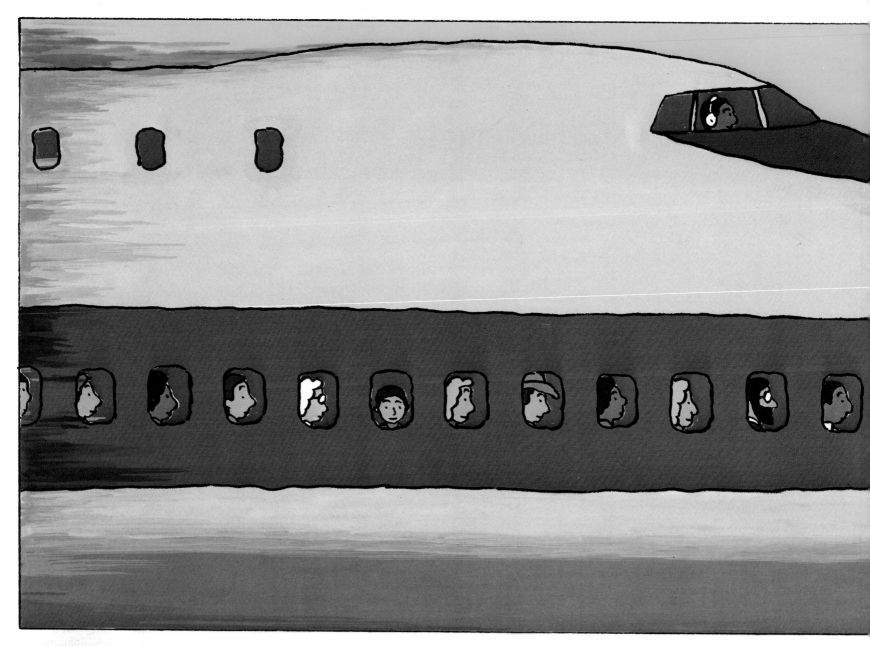

They roar down the runway

faster and faster,

then up in the air.

They are on their way.